Table of Contents

INTRODUCTION

Golf is a popular sport among Americans, a sport that is not practiced by everyone, because it involves substantial costs and also the techniques you have to adopt are not easy to learn. In the book, we want to unravel the secrets of golf so that we can learn together everything that is more interesting in this sport. As a result, it has many terms, rules, and regulations that can be tough to learn at first. This is why this book is highly essential.

Although golf can be difficult while you're still learning proper technique, the game can be very enjoyable as you master your skills. One aspect that makes golf challenging is that even small details can have a big impact on your shot. It all starts with your swing. If you're slicing or hooking your ball, if you're just not getting the right yardage out of your shot, or if you've never hit a golf ball in your life, here's the skinny on how to get the best out of your golf swing.

CHAPTER ONE

Origin and History

While the modern game of golf originated in 15th-century Scotland, the game's ancient origins are unclear and much debated. Some historians trace the sport back to the Roman game of paganica, in which participants used a bent stick to hit a stuffed leather ball. One theory asserts that paganica spread throughout Europe as the Romans conquered most of the continent, during the first century BC, and eventually evolved into the modern game.

Another early game that resembled modern golf was known as cambuca in England and chambot in France. The Persian game chowkan is another possible ancient origin, albeit being more polo-like. In addition, kolven (a game involving a ball and curved bats) was played annually in Loenen, Netherlands, beginning in 1297, to commemorate the capture of the assassin of Floris V, a year earlier.

The modern game originated in Scotland, where the first written record of golf is James II's banning of the game in 1457, as an unwelcome distraction to learning archery.

James IV lifted the ban in 1502 when he became a golfer himself, with golf clubs first recorded in 1503–1504: "For golf clubbes and balles to the King that he playit with". To many golfers, the Old Course at St Andrews, a links course dating to before 1574, is considered to be a site of pilgrimage. In 1764, the standard 18-hole golf course was created at St Andrews when members modified the course from 22 to 18 holes. Golf is documented as being played on Musselburgh Links, East Lothian, Scotland as early as 2 March 1672, which is certified as the oldest golf course in the world by Guinness World Records. The oldest surviving rules of golf were compiled in March 1744 for the Company of Gentlemen Golfers, later renamed The Honourable Company of Edinburgh Golfers, which was played at Leith, Scotland. The world's oldest golf tournament in existence, and golf's first major, is The Open Championship, which was first played on 17 October 1860 at Prestwick Golf Club, in Ayrshire, Scotland, with Scottish golfers winning the earliest majors. Two Scotsmen from Dunfermline, John Reid and Robert Lockhart, first demonstrated golf in the U.S. by setting up a hole in an orchard in 1888, with Reid setting up America's first golf club the same year, Saint Andrew's Golf Club in Yonkers, New York.

Golf Course

A golf course consists of either 9 or 18 holes, each with a teeing ground or "tee box" that is set off by two markers showing the bounds of the legal tee area, fairway, rough and other hazards, and the putting green surrounded by the fringe with the pin (normally a flagstick) and cup.

The levels of grass are varied to increase difficulty, or to allow for putting in the case of the green. While many holes are designed with a direct line-of-sight from the teeing area to the green, some holes may bend either to the left or to the right. This is commonly called a "dogleg", in reference to a dog's knee. The hole is called a "dogleg left" if the hole angles leftwards and "dogleg right" if it bends right. Sometimes, a hole's direction may bend twice; this is called a "double dogleg".

A regular golf course consists of 18 holes, but nine-hole courses are common and can be played twice through for a full round of 18 holes. Early Scottish golf courses were primarily laid out on links land, soil-covered sand dunes directly inland from beaches. The word "links" derives from the Scots language and the Old English word hlinc ("rising ground, ridge"): traditionally these are coastal sand dunes but sometimes open parkland. This gave rise to the term "golf links", particularly applied to seaside courses and those built on naturally sandy soil inland.

How do we describe the game?

Golf is a sport rich in tradition and history. As a result, it has many terms, rules, and regulations that can be tough to learn at first. This is why our golf experts at our South Florida Golf Course compiled a list of common golf terms, rules, etiquette, tournaments, and equipment so that you show up to the course prepared. Golf is a club-and-ball sport in which players use various clubs to hit balls into a series of holes on a course in as few strokes as possible.

Golf, unlike most ball games, cannot and does not utilize a standardized playing area, and coping with the varied terrains encountered on different courses is a key part of the game. The game at the usual level is played on a course with an arranged progression of 18 holes, though recreational courses can be smaller, often having nine holes. Each hole on the course must contain a teeing ground to start from, and a putting green containing the actual hole or cup 4+1/4 inches (11 cm) in diameter. There are other standard forms of terrain in between, such as the fairway, rough (long grass), bunkers (or "sand traps"), and various hazards (water, rocks) but each hole on a course is unique in its specific layout and arrangement. Golf is played for the lowest number of strokes by an individual, known as stroke play, or the lowest score on the most individual holes in a complete round by an individual or team, known as match play. Stroke play is the most commonly seen format at all levels, but most especially at the elite level.

The modern game of golf originated in 15th century Scotland. The 18-hole round was created at the Old Course at St Andrews in 1764. Golf's first major, and the world's oldest tournament in existence, is The Open Championship, also known as the British Open, which was first played in 1860 at the Prestwick Golf Club in Ayrshire, Scotland. This is one of the four major championships in men's professional golf, the other three being played in the United States: The Masters, the U.S. Open, and the PGA Championship.

Playing the Game

Every round of golf is based on playing a number of holes in a given order. A "round" typically consists of 18 holes that are played in the order determined by the course layout. Each hole is played once in the round on a standard course of 18 holes. The game can be played by any number of people, although a typical group playing will have 1-4 people playing the round. The typical amount of time required for pace of play for a 9-hole round is two hours and four hours for an 18-hole round.

Playing a hole on a golf course is initiated by putting a ball into play by striking it with a club on the teeing ground (also called the tee box, or simply the tee). For this first shot on each hole, it is allowed but not required for the golfer to place the ball on a tee prior to striking it. A tee is a small peg that can be used to elevate the ball slightly above the ground up to a few centimetres high. Tees are commonly made of wood but may be constructed of any material, including plastic. Traditionally, golfers used mounds of sand to elevate the ball, and containers of sand were provided for the purpose. A few courses still require sand to be used instead of peg tees, to reduce litter and reduce damage to the teeing ground. Tees help reduce the interference of the ground or grass on the movement of the club making the ball easier to hit, and also places the ball in the very centre of the striking face of the club (the "sweet spot") for better distance.

When the initial shot on a hole is intended to move the ball a long distance, typically more than 225 yards (210 m), the shot is commonly called a "drive" and is generally made with a long-shafted, large-headed wood club called a "driver". Shorter holes may be initiated with other clubs, such as higher-numbered woods or irons. Once the ball comes to rest, the golfer strikes it again as many times as necessary using shots that are variously known as a "lay-up", an "approach", a "pitch", or a "chip", until the ball reaches the green, where he or she then "putts" the ball into the hole (commonly called "sinking the putt" or "holing out"). The goal of getting the ball into the hole ("holing" the ball) in as few strokes as possible may be impeded by obstacles such as areas of longer grass called "rough" (usually found alongside fairways), which both slows any ball that contacts it and makes it harder to advance a ball that has stopped on it; "doglegs", which are changes in the direction of the fairway that often require shorter shots to play around them; bunkers (or sand traps); and water hazards such as ponds or streams.

In stroke play competitions played according to strict rules, each player plays their ball until it is holed no matter how many strokes that may take. In match play it is acceptable to simply pick up one's ball and "surrender the hole" after enough strokes have been made by a player that it is mathematically impossible for the player to win the hole. It is also acceptable in informal stroke play to surrender the hole after hitting three strokes more than the "par" rating of the hole (a "triple bogey" - see below); while technically a violation of Rule 3–2, this practice speeds play as a courtesy to others, and avoids "runaway scores", excessive frustration and injuries caused by overexertion.

The total distance from the first teeing ground to the 18th green can be quite long; total yardages "through the green" can be in excess of 7,000 yards (6.4 km), and when adding in the travel distance between the green of one hole and the tee of the next, even skilled players may easily travel five miles (8 km) or more during a round. At some courses, electric golf carts are used to travel between shots, which can speed-up play and allows participation by individuals unable to walk a whole round. On other courses players generally walk the course, either carrying their bag using a shoulder strap or using a "golf trolley" for their bag. These trolleys may or may not be battery assisted. At many amateur tournaments including U.S. high school and college play, players are required to walk and to carry their own bags, but at the professional and top amateur level, as well as at high-level private clubs, players may be accompanied by caddies, who carry and manage the players' equipment and who are allowed by the rules to give advice on the play of the course. A caddie's advice can only be given to the player or players for whom the caddie is working, and not to other competing players.

The first 18-hole golf course in the United States was on a sheep farm in Downers Grove, Illinois, in 1892. The course is still there today.

Rules and Regulations

The rules of golf are internationally standardised and are jointly governed by The R&A, spun off in 2004 from The Royal and Ancient Golf Club of St Andrews (founded 1754), and the United States Golf Association (USGA). With the aim of simplifying the rules, in 2017 the USGA and R&A undertook a complete rewrite. The new rule book came into effect in January 2019.

Play the ball as it lies, play the course as you find it, and if you cannot do either, do what is fair.

There are strict regulations regarding the amateur status of golfers. Essentially, anybody who has ever received payment or compensation for giving instruction, or played golf for money, is not considered an amateur and may not participate in competitions limited solely to amateurs. However, amateur golfers may receive expenses that comply with strict guidelines and they may accept non-cash prizes within the limits established by the Rules of Amateur Status. In addition to the officially printed rules, golfers also abide by a set of guidelines called golf etiquette. Etiquette guidelines cover matters such as safety, fairness, pace of play, and a player's obligation to contribute to the care of the course. Though there are no penalties for breach of etiquette rules, players generally follow the rules of golf etiquette in an effort to improve everyone's playing experience.

Penalties

Penalty strokes are incurred in certain situations and are counted towards a player's score as if there were extra swing(s) at the ball. Either one or two strokes are added for most rule infractions or for taking relief from various situations, with the "general penalty" defined as two-strokes, and disqualification for severe or repeated rule breaches. Examples include:

- A lost ball or a ball hit out of bounds (OB) results in a penalty of one stroke and distance (Rule 18.2).

- With the exception of certain circumstances, a one-stroke penalty is assessed if a player causes their ball to move (Rule 9.4).

- A one-stroke penalty is assessed if a player elects to take relief when their ball comes to rest within a red or yellow penalty area (Rule 17), or from an unplayable lie (Rule 19).

- A two-stroke penalty is incurred for making a stroke at the wrong ball (Rule 6.3c).

- A two-stroke penalty is incurred for hitting a fellow player's ball if both balls lay on the green prior to the stroke (Rule 11.1a).

- Disqualification can result from cheating, signing for a lower score, or failing to adhere to one or more rules that lead to improper play.

Equipment

Golf clubs are used to hit the golf ball. Each club is composed of a shaft with a lance (or "grip") on the top end and a club head on the bottom. Long clubs, which have a lower amount of degree loft, are those meant to propel the ball a comparatively longer distance, and short clubs a higher degree of loft and a comparatively shorter distance. The actual physical length of each club is longer or shorter, depending on the distance the club is intended to propel the ball.

Golf clubs have traditionally been arranged into three basic types. Woods are large-headed, long-shafted clubs meant to propel the ball a long distance from relatively "open" lies, such as the teeing ground and fairway. Of particular importance is the driver or "1-wood", which is the lowest lofted wood club, and in modern times has become highly specialized for making extremely long-distance tee shots, up to 300 yards (270 m), or more, in a professional golfer's hands. Traditionally these clubs had heads made of a hardwood, hence the name, but virtually all modern woods are now made of metal such as titanium, or of composite materials. Irons are shorter-shafted clubs with a metal head primarily consisting of a flat, angled striking face. Traditionally the clubhead was forged from iron; modern iron clubheads are investment-cast from a steel alloy. Irons of varying loft are used for a variety of shots from virtually anywhere on the course, but most often for shorter-distance shots approaching the green, or to get the ball out of tricky lies such as sand traps. The third class is the putter, which evolved from the irons to create a low-lofted, balanced club designed to roll the ball along the green and into the hole. Putters are virtually always used on the green or in the surrounding rough/fringe. A fourth class, called hybrids, evolved as a cross between woods and irons, and are typically seen replacing the low-lofted irons with a club that provides similar distance, but a higher launch angle and a more forgiving nature.

A maximum of 14 clubs is allowed in a player's bag at one time during a stipulated round. The choice of clubs is at the golfer's discretion, although every club must be constructed in accordance with parameters outlined in the rules. (Clubs that meet these parameters are usually called "conforming".) Violation of these rules can result in disqualification.

The exact shot hit at any given time on a golf course, and which club is used to accomplish the shot, are always completely at the discretion of the golfer; in other words, there is no restriction whatsoever on which club a golfer may or may not use at any time for any shot.

Golf balls are spherical, usually white (although other colours are allowed), and minutely pock-marked by dimples that decrease aerodynamic drag by increasing air turbulence around the ball in motion, which delays "boundary layer" separation and reduces the drag-inducing "wake" behind the ball, thereby allowing the ball to fly farther. The combination of a soft "boundary layer" and a hard "core" enables both distance and spin.

A tee is allowed only for the first stroke on each hole, unless the player must hit a provisional tee shot or replay their first shot from the tee. Many golfers wear golf shoes with metal or plastic spikes designed to increase traction, thus allowing for longer and more accurate shots.

A golf bag is used to transport golf clubs and the player's other or personal equipment. Golf bags have several pockets designed for carrying equipment and supplies such as tees, balls, and gloves. Golf bags can be carried, pulled on a trolley or harnessed to a motorized golf cart during play. Golf bags usually have both a hand strap and shoulder strap for carrying, others may be carried over both shoulders like a backpack, and often bags have retractable legs that allow the bag to stand upright when at rest.

Common Golf Terms

Golf Course Terms

Golf Tee – The wooden peg you place your golf ball on at the start of the hole.

Golf Tee Box – The area in which you first play the ball at the start of the hole.

Fairway – The part of the golf course that leads to the green, usually where putting takes place.

The green – The soft, plush ground surrounding the hole.

The rough – The wild area on either side of the fairway. This area is often filled with trees and long grass.

Bunker – A sand–filled ditch that usually surrounds the green.

Hazard – Streams, ponds, bunkers, trees. Anything that comes between you and successfully getting the golf ball in the hole.

Stroke Mechanics

The golf swing is outwardly similar to many other motions involving swinging a tool or playing implement, such as an axe or a baseball bat. However, unlike many of these motions, the result of the swing is highly dependent on several sub-motions being properly aligned and timed. These ensure that the club travels up to the ball in line with the desired path; that the clubface is in line with the swing path; and that the ball hits the centre or "sweet spot" of the clubface. The ability to do this consistently, across a complete set of clubs with a wide range of shaft lengths and clubface areas, is a key skill for any golfer, and takes a significant effort to achieve.

Stance

Stance refers to how the golfer positions themselves in order to play a stroke; it is fundamentally important in being able to play a stroke effectively. The stance adopted is determined by what stroke is being played. All stances involve a slight crouch. This allows for a more efficient striking posture whilst also isometrically preloading the muscles of the legs and core; this allows the stroke to be played more dynamically and with a greater level of overall control. When adopting their stance golfers start with the non-dominant side of the body facing the target (for a right-hander, the target is to their left). Setting the stance in regard to the position of the ball, and placing the clubhead behind the ball, is known as being at address; when in this position the player's body and the centerline of the club face are positioned parallel to the desired line of travel, with the feet either perpendicular to that line or slightly splayed outward. The feet are commonly shoulder-width apart for middle irons and putters, narrower for short irons and wider for long irons and woods. The ball is typically positioned more to the "front" of the player's stance (closer to the leading foot) for lower-lofted clubs, with the usual ball position for a drive being just behind the arch of the leading foot. The ball is placed further "back" in the player's stance (toward the trailing foot) as the loft of the club to be used increases. Most iron shots and putts are made with the ball roughly centered in the stance, while a few mid- and short-iron shots are made with the ball slightly behind the centre of the stance to ensure consistent contact between the ball and clubface, so the ball is on its way before the club continues down into the turf.

Strokes

The golfer chooses a golf club, grip, and stroke appropriate to the distance:

The "drive" or "full swing" is used on the teeing ground and fairway, typically with a wood or long iron, to produce the maximum distance capable with the club. In the extreme, the windup can end with the shaft of the club parallel to the ground above the player's shoulders.

The "approach" or "3/4 swing" is used in medium- and long-distance situations where an exact distance and good accuracy is preferable to maximum possible distance, such as to place the ball on the green or "lay up" in front of a hazard. The windup or "backswing" of such a shot typically ends up with the shaft of the club pointing straight upwards or slightly towards the player.

The "chip" or "half-swing" is used for relatively short-distance shots near the green, with high-lofted irons and wedges. The goal of the chip is to land the ball safely on the green, allowing it to roll out towards the hole. It can also be used from other places to accurately position the ball into a more advantageous lie. The backswing typically ends with the head of the club between hip and head height.

The "putt" is used in short-distance shots on or near the green, typically made with the eponymous "putter", although similar strokes can be made with medium to high-numbered irons to carry a short distance in the air and then roll (a "bump and run"). The backswing and follow-through of the putt are both abbreviated compared to other strokes, with the head of the club rarely rising above the knee. The goal of the putt is usually to put the ball in the hole, although a long-distance putt may be called a "lag" and is made with the primary intention of simply closing distance to the hole or otherwise placing the ball advantageously.

Having chosen a club and stroke to produce the desired distance, the player addresses the ball by taking their stance to the side of it and (except when the ball lies in a hazard) grounding the club behind the ball. The golfer then takes their backswing, rotating the club, their arms and their upper body away from the ball, and then begins their swing, bringing the clubhead back down and around to hit the ball. A proper golf swing is a complex combination of motions, and slight variations in posture or positioning can make a great deal of difference in how well the ball is hit and how straight it travels. The general goal of a player making a full swing is to propel the clubhead as fast as possible while maintaining a single "plane" of motion of the club and clubhead, to send the clubhead into the ball along the desired path of travel and with the clubhead also pointing that direction.

Accuracy and consistency are typically stressed over pure distance. A player with a straight drive that travels only 220 yards (200 m) will nevertheless be able to accurately place the ball into a favourable lie on the fairway, and can make up for the lesser distance of any given club by simply using "more club" (a lower loft) on their tee shot or on subsequent fairway and approach shots. However, a golfer with a drive that may go 280 yards (260 m) but often does not fly straight will be less able to position their ball advantageously; the ball may "hook", "pull", "draw", "fade", "push" or "slice" off the intended line and land out of bounds or in the rough or hazards, and thus the player will require many more strokes to hole out.

Musculature

A golf stroke uses the muscles of the core (especially erector spinae muscles and latissimus dorsi muscle when turning), hamstring, shoulder, and wrist. Stronger muscles in the wrist can prevent them from being twisted during swings, whilst stronger shoulders increase the turning force. Weak wrists can also transmit the force to elbows and even neck and lead to injury. (When a muscle contracts, it pulls equally from both ends and, to have movement at only one end of the muscle, other muscles must come into play to stabilize the bone to which the other end of the muscle is attached.) Golf is a unilateral exercise that can break body balances, requiring exercises to keep the balance in muscles.

Types of putting

Putting is considered to be the most important component of the game of golf. As the game of golf has evolved, there have been many different putting techniques and grips that have been devised to give golfers the best chance to make putts. When the game originated, golfers would putt with their dominant hand on the bottom of the grip and their weak hand on top of the grip. This grip and putting style is known as "conventional". There are many variations of conventional including overlap, where the golfer overlaps the off hand index finger onto off the dominant pinky; interlock, where the offhand index finger interlocks with the dominant pinky and ring finger; double or triple overlap and so on. Recently, "cross handed" putting has become a popular trend amongst professional golfers and amateurs. Cross handed putting is the idea that the dominant hand is on top of the grip where the weak hand is on the bottom. This grip restricts the motion in your dominant hand and eliminates the possibility of wrist breakdowns through the putting stroke.

Other notable putting styles include "the claw", a style that has the grip directly in between the thumb and index finger of the dominant hand while the palm faces the target. The weak hand placed normally on the putter. Anchored putting, a style that requires a longer putter shaft that can be anchored into the player's stomach or below the chin; the idea is to stabilize one end of the putter thus creating a more consistent pendulum stroke. This style has been banned on professional circuits since 2016.

Golf Scoring Terms

Ace – A hole in one.

Eagle – 2 strokes under par.

Birdie – 1 stroke under par (sometimes called a double eagle).

Par – The standard number of strokes it should take to get the golf ball from the tee to the hole.

Bogey – 1 stroke above par.

Double Bogey – 2 strokes above par.

Triple Bogey – 3 strokes above par.

Scoring

The goal is to play as few strokes per round as possible. A golfer's number of strokes in a hole, course, or tournament is compared to its respective par score, and is then reported either as the number that the golfer was "under-" or "over-par", or if it was "equal to par". A hole in one (or an "ace") occurs when a golfer sinks their ball into the cup with their first stroke from the tee. Common scores for a hole also have specific terms.

There are two basic forms of golf play, match play and stroke play. Stroke play is more popular.

Match play

Two players (or two teams) play each hole as a separate contest against each other in what is called match play. The party with the lower score wins that hole, or if the scores of both players or teams are equal the hole is "halved" (or tied). The game is won by the party that wins more holes than the other. In the case that one team or player has taken a lead that cannot be overcome in the number of holes remaining to be played, the match is deemed to be won by the party in the lead, and the remainder of the holes are not played. For example, if one party already has a lead of six holes, and only five holes remain to be played on the course, the match is over and the winning party is deemed to have won "6 & 5". At any given point, if the lead is equal to the number of holes remaining, the party leading the match is said to be "dormie", and the match is continued until the party increases the lead by one hole or ties any of the remaining holes, thereby winning the match, or until the match ends in a tie with the lead player's opponent winning all remaining holes. When the game is tied after the predetermined number of holes have been played, it may be continued until one side takes a one-hole lead.

Stroke play

The score achieved for each and every hole of the round or tournament is added to produce the total score, and the player with the lowest score wins in stroke play. Stroke play is the game most commonly played by professional golfers. If there is a tie after the regulation number of holes in a professional tournament, a playoff takes place between all tied players. Playoffs either are sudden death or employ a pre-determined number of holes, anywhere from three to a full 18. In sudden death, a player who scores lower on a hole than all of their opponents wins the match. If at least two players remain tied after such a playoff using a pre-determined number of holes, then play continues in sudden death format, where the first player to win a hole wins the tournament.

1. Hands & Arms Swing

If you initiate limited lower body rotation during your swing, it leads to a reliance on your hands and arms. This is known as the hands and arms swing. Although it can help you hinge the golf club and optimize club head speed, it exposes you to inaccurate shots.

The lack of hip turn typically results in golfers producing a steep angle of attack. This leaves you susceptible to topping your shot or a slice. Plus, it is difficult to bring your club onto its swing plane and can cause you to leave your clubface open at impact. That prompts left to right sidespin, inducing a slice.

Mark Crossfield explains that an amateur golfer hits better iron shots than woods with this swing. The steep angle of attack requires you to pick the clubhead up before impact to avoid hitting behind the ball.

When the ball position is forward in your stance with a driver swing, you might struggle to get the club on plane for impact. When you get your shaft is in position at the bottom of your downswing, the corrective action reduces momentum and power at impact

Pros

- The additional time in the air generates increased clubhead speed
- Helps players remain centered during their swing
- Produces a high trajectory
- Suited to taller golfers
- Allows more freedom of movement

Cons

- Susceptible to topping your shot
- It is hard to control the clubhead at the top of the swing, sending it off plane.
- It can cause imbalance by shifting weight in the wrong direction at impact and on your follow-through.

I explained the mechanics of the closed coil golf swing in a previous post, so I will be brief. Simply put, this swing helps you maximize spring when you reach the top of the backswing, prompting optimal force on your downswing.

The additional speed generated when coiling promotes a superior coefficient of restitution (COR) at impact for optimal ball speed. Therefore you enjoy a consistent mid to high launch for improved yardage.

Unlike the hands and arms swing, the closed coil set-up demands optimal rotation of the hips to generate the necessary power. In addition, failure to coil sufficiently could lead your club off plane, resulting in an off-center strike.

Golf coach Dan Whittaker provides an informative visual breakdown explaining how to execute a closed coil swing.

Pros

- Optimizes power
- Suited to senior players as it carries less injury risk than other swings

- Promotes increased COR at impact.

- It makes it easy for casual golfers to get the club on plane for increased accuracy.

- Encourages rapid ball speed

- You need to maximize your lower body's rotation to get your clubface square at impact.

- The clubhead's at the top of your backswing can feel awkward. That may cause you to try and correct the path and come over the top.

3. Inside-Out Swing

The inside-out golf swing refers to the path your golf club journeys from takeaway through impact. Contrary to the closed coil swing, which focuses on hip rotation, this swing relies heavily on your torso.

On your takeaway, the combination of the rotation of your hips and upper body takes the clubhead inside. At the top of your backswing, shift your weight to your right shoulder and left leg. That prompts the clubhead to follow an outside path to the ball, with minor lag.

Producing sufficient rotation leads to a square or marginally closed clubface at impact. However, an off-tempo swing prevents you from bringing the club on plane when the shaft is parallel to the ground. As a result, you may angle the clubface incorrectly and prompt and slice or a hook.

Overall, the inside-out golf swing best suits those players looking to induce a draw or combat a slice.

Pros

- Promotes straighter ball flight
- Helps you hit a draw shape
- Delivers increased distance over an outside-in swing.
- Reduces the risk of a slice

Cons

- If your rhythm is off and you clear your hips too quickly, your clubface may close at impact and prompt a hook.
- Inadequate rotation can cause your clubface to remain open at impact leading to a slice.

The outside-in-swing is commonly employed by amateurs and brings a host of risks. It reduces hip and shoulder rotation, lowering power at impact. Furthermore, it leads to you coming over the top and increases the risk of topping your shot.

In addition, the outside-in swing path may cause you to cut across your ball and generate right to left spin. That leads to a fade or a slice.

It is not the most efficient swing by any means. But, professional golfers may apply it when they are purposefully trying to hit a fade. Overall, there are more cons than advantages to using the inside-out golf swing.

Pros
- Perfect swing to purposefully hit a fade
- It can help you increase your clubhead speed

Cons
- Causes slices
- Reduces COR
- Leaves you at risk of topping your shots

5. One-Plane Swing

A single plane swing (aka the one-plane swing) is ideal for the average golfer looking to remove the complexities from their swing. Golfweek explains that a two-plane swing requires more wrists and hands work to optimize power. However, a one-plane swing sees your body work as a unit.

At the top of your backswing, your arms should remain on the same plane as your shoulders. In addition, your right foot must remain grounded for supreme stability.

The one-plane swing is easy for beginners because of the transition from the top of your backswing down. Since your shoulders and arms are level, you needn't wait to lower the club. That means you can proceed with your downswing and shift your weight to your left foot the moment you reach the top.

Therefore, you enjoy a free-flowing swing rhythm that generates supreme clubhead speed and power on your downswing. That leads to optimal distance off the tee and on approach.

Another advantage of the one-plane swing is the consistency that it gives you. Whether you are swinging a wedge or a driver, you can repeat the same backswing and follow through for a clean strike. The only element that changes is whether you position the ball closer to your left foot or the center of your stance.

Pros

- Provides consistency
- Less complex than a two-plane swing
- Easier to keep the club on plane throughout the swing
- Designed to combat slices

Cons

- Keeping your left arm close to your chest can cause you to close the clubface before impact and hook your shot.

Common Golf Etiquette

Although golf is a competitive sport, there are general guidelines and etiquette that are expected to be followed on the course. While not found in the official rule book, these guidelines are expected to be followed at all golf courses, including our Deerfield Beach, Florida course.

Don't talk during someone's backswing.

Don't walk through someone else's line (the line from their ball to the hole).

Don't hit the ball into the group ahead of you. Wait for them to finish.

If a group behind you is playing faster, consider letting them go first at the next hole.

Avoid angry outbursts.

What Is a Golf Handicap?

A golf handicap is a number that represents the skill level of a golfer. A golf handicap will vary from player to player and is based on previous scores achieved. The formula for calculating your golf score can change from year to year. You can find the latest handicap calculator on the official USGA website here. In order to calculate your handicap, you will need to have golfed at least a 9 or 18-hole course and have your scorecard handy.

What, When, and Where Are the Major Professional Golf Tournaments Held?

A great way to learn more about the game of golf is to watch the professionals. Watching professional players golf can also give you pointers on your own game and set an example for yourself. The major golf tournaments are as follows:

- The Four Majors (Grand Slam: win all four in a calendar year. Tiger Slam: hold all four at one time).
- The Masters – First week of April and always held at the same place every year: the Augusta National Golf Club.
- The US Open – Mid-June and held at various golf courses around the United States.

- The Open – Mid-July and held at various golf courses around the United Kingdom. Also referred to as the British Open.
- PGA Championship – Mid-August and held on the eastern side of the United States.
- The Ryder Cup – End of September. The Ryder Cup is the most important team golf tournament. The tournament is between the United States and Europe.
- The Barclays – Mid-June and held at various golf courses, especially around the New York area.
- The Travelers – Late June, at the TPC River Highlands course.

Put Your Golf Knowledge to the Test

Our Deer Creek Golf Course is open to the public, and to any and all golfers, from beginners to professionals. There are no handicap requirements to playing, and we only ask that you respect the golf etiquette outlined above. Check out our tee times and rates for our renowned course.

This book offer newbies to golf a general overview of the form and function of each type of golf club.

Meet the Woods

The category of golf clubs called "woods" includes the driver and the fairway woods. (They are called woods even though their clubheads are no longer made of wood.) The woods are the clubs with the largest heads (typically hollow, extending a few inches from side-to-side and a few inches from front to back, with rounded lines) and with the longest shafts. Golfers can swing them the fastest, and they are used for the longest shots, including strokes played from the teeing ground.

Meet the Irons

Irons come in numbered sets, usually ranging from 3-iron through 9-iron or pitching wedge. They have smaller clubheads than woods, especially front to back where they are comparitively very thin (leading to one of their nicknames: "blades"). Most irons have solid heads, although some are hollow. Irons have angled faces (called "loft") etched with grooves that help grip the golf ball and impart spin. They are generally used on shots from the fairway, or for tee shots on short holes.

As the number of an iron goes up (5-iron, 6-iron, etc.), the loft increases while the length of the shaft decreases.

Meet the Hybrids

Hybrid clubs are the newest category of golf club. They became mainstream only around the turn of the 21st century, although they existed for many years prior to that. Think of the clubhead of a hybrid as a cross between a wood and an iron. Hence the name "hybrid" (they are also sometimes called utility clubs or rescue clubs). Hybrids are numbered like irons are (e.g., 2-hybrid, 3-hybrid, etc.), and the number corresponds to the iron they replace. That's because hybrids are considered "iron-replacement clubs," meaning that many golfers find them easier to hit than the irons they replace. But if a golfer uses hybrids, it is most likely as a replacement for the long irons (2-, 3-, 4- or 5-irons).

Meet the Wedges

The category of wedges includes the pitching wedge, gap wedge, sand wedge and lob wedge. Wedges are their own type of golf club, but also are a sub-set of irons because they have the same clubheads as irons, just more severely angled for more loft. The wedges are the highest-lofted golf clubs. They are used for shorter approach shots into greens, for chips and pitches around greens, and for playing out of sand bunkers.

Meet the Putter

Putters are the most-specialized golf clubs, and the type of club that comes in the widest varieties of shapes and sizes. Putters are used for, well, putting. They are the clubs golfers use on the putting greens, for the last strokes played on a golf hole - for knocking the ball into the hole. There are more varieties of putters on the market than any other club. That may be because choosing a putter is a very personal process. There is no "right" putter. There is simply the putter that is right for you. Putters generally come in three styles of clubhead, and three varieties of lengths.

Clubheads: Clubheads can be a traditional blade; a heel-toe clubhead; or a mallet clubhead. A traditional blade is narrow and shallow, typically with the shaft entering at the heel (although sometimes center-shafted). Heel-toe putters have the same general shape as blades, but with extra weight at the heel and toe to add perimeter weighting, and with other design tricks to help make the clubs more "forgiving" on mishits. Mallet putters have large clubheads that maximize that forgiveness of poor contact. Mallets come in a variety of shapes and sizes, some very large and quite unusual.

Lengths: Standard-length putters, often referred to as "conventional putters," range from around 32 to 36 inches long, from one end to the other. Standard, or conventional, length is the most popular and is the length that beginners should start with. Belly putters are those whose length causes the grip-end to come up to - you guessed it - the golfer's belly. And long putters (a k a broomstick putters) are in the upper 40-inch, lower 50-inch range, allowing the golfer to stand more upright.

Personality: But what putters boil down to is personal choice. If it feels good to you when you are using a putter, then that putter will probably work just fine. So much of putting is confidence, so having a putter that feels good, that appeals to your eye, that you simply like, can only be a good thing.

All putters, regardless of size or shape, are designed to start the ball rolling smoothly, with a minimum of backspin to avoid skipping or skidding. Almost all putters do have a small amount of loft (typically 3 or 4 degrees).

Golf Playing and Scoring formats

There are many variations in scoring and playing formats in the game of golf, some officially defined in the Rules of Golf. Variations include the popular Stableford scoring system, and various team formats. Some common and popular examples are listed below.

There are also variations on the usual starting procedure where everyone begins from the first tee and plays all holes in order, though to the eighteenth. In large field tournaments, especially on professional tours, a two tee start is commonplace, where the field will be split between starting on the first tee and the tenth tee (sometimes the eighth or eleventh depending on proximity to the clubhouse). Shotgun starts are mainly used for amateur tournament or society play. In this variant, each of the groups playing starts their game on a different hole, allowing for all players to start and end their round at roughly the same time. For example, a group starting on hole 5 will play through to the 18th hole and continue with hole 1, ending their round on hole 4.

Bogey or Par competition

A bogey or par competition is a scoring format sometimes seen in informal tournaments. Its scoring is similar to match play, except each player compares their hole score to the hole's par rating instead of the score of another player. The player "wins" the hole if they score a birdie or better, they "lose" the hole if they score a bogey or worse, and they "halve" the hole by scoring par. By recording only this simple win-loss-halve score on the sheet, a player can shrug off a very poorly-played hole with a simple "-" mark and move on. As used in competitions, the player or pair with the best win-loss "differential" wins the competition.

Stableford

The Stableford system is a simplification of stroke play that awards players points based on their score relative to the hole's par; the score for a hole is calculated by taking the par score, adding 2, then subtracting the player's hole score, making the result zero if negative. Alternately stated, a double bogey or worse is zero points, a bogey is worth one point, par is two, a birdie three, an eagle four, and so on. The advantages of this system over stroke play are a more natural "higher is better" scoring, the ability to compare Stableford scores between plays on courses with different total par scores (scoring an "even" in stroke play will always give a Stableford score of 36), discouraging the tendency to abandon the entire game after playing a particularly bad hole (a novice playing by strict rules may score as high as an 8 or 10 on a single difficult hole; their Stableford score for the hole would be zero, which puts them only two points behind par no matter how badly they played), and the ability to simply pick up one's ball once it is impossible to score any points for the hole, which speeds play.

The USGA and R&A sanction a "Modified Stableford" system for scratch players, which makes par worth zero, a birdie worth 2, eagle 5 and double-eagle 8, while a bogey is a penalty of −1 and a double-bogey or worse −3. As with the original system, the highest score wins the game, and terrible scores on one or two holes will not ruin a player's overall score, but this system rewards "bogey-birdie" play more than the original, encouraging golfers to try to make riskier birdie putt or eagle chipshots instead of simply parring each hole.

Foursomes (also known as Alternate Shot): defined in Rule 22, this is played in pairs, in which each team has only one ball and players alternate playing it. For example, if players "A" and "B" form a team, "A" tees off on the first hole, "B" will play the second shot, "A" the third, and so on until the hole is finished. On the second hole, "B" will tee off (regardless who played the last putt on the first hole), then "A" plays the second shot, and so on. Foursomes can be played as match play or stroke play.

Greensomes (also known as Scotch Foursomes): also called modified alternate shot, this is played in pairs; both players tee off, and then pick the best shot. The player who did not shoot the best first shot plays the second shot. The play then alternates as in a foursome. A variant of greensome is sometimes played where the opposing team chooses which of their opponent's tee shots the opponents should use.

Four-ball: defined in Rules 23, this is also played in pairs, but every each plays their own ball and for each team, the lower score on each hole counts. Four-ball can be played as match play or stroke play.

Scramble: also known as ambrose or best-shot; each player in a team tees off on each hole, and the players decide which shot was best. Every player then plays their second shot from within a clublength of where the best shot has come to rest (and no closer to the hole), and the procedure is repeated until the hole is finished. This system is very common at informal tournaments such as for charity, as it speeds play (due to the reduced number of shots taken from bad lies), allows teams of varying sizes, and allows players of widely varying skill levels to participate without profoundly affecting team score.

Best-ball: like four-ball, each player plays the hole as normal, but the lowest score of all the players on the team counts as the team's score for the hole. There are many variations on this format, which count a different number of scores on each hole.

A handicap is a numerical measure of a golfer's potential scoring ability over 18 holes. It is used to enable players of widely varying abilities to compete against one another. Better players are those with the lowest handicaps, and someone with a handicap of 0 or less is often referred to as a scratch golfer. Handicap systems vary throughout the world and use different methods to assess courses and calculate handicaps. In order to address difficulties in translating between these systems the USGA and The R&A, working with the various existing handicapping authorities, devised a new World Handicap System which is set to be introduced globally starting in 2020.

Golf courses are assessed and rated according to the average good score of a scratch golfer, taking into account a multitude of factors affecting play, such as length, obstacles, undulations, etc. A player's handicap gives an indication of the number of strokes above this course rating that the player will make over the course of an "average best" round of golf, i.e. scoring near their potential, above average. Lower handicap players are generally the most consistent, so can be expected to play to this standard or better more often than higher handicappers. Some handicap systems also account for differences in scoring difficulty between low and high handicap golfer. They do this by means of assessing and rating courses according to the average good score of a "bogey golfer", a player with a handicap of around 20. This is used with the course rating to calculate a slope rating, which is used to adjust golfer's handicap to produce a playing handicap for the course and set of tees being used.

Handicap systems have potential for abuse by players who may intentionally play badly to increase their handicap (sandbagging) before playing to their potential at an important event with a valuable prize. For this reason, handicaps are not used in professional golf, but they can still be calculated and used along with other criteria to determine the relative strengths of various professional players. Touring professionals, being the best of the best, have negative handicaps; they can be expected, more often than not, to score lower than the Course Rating on any course.

1) Golf Grip Size (Outer Diameter)

Golf grips come in 6 different "sizes" which refer to outer diameter: Standard, Midsize, Oversize/Jumbo, Undersize, and Junior. Every manufacture has a slightly different definition of diameter sizing, but in general Standard grips are around 1" in diameter. Midsize and Oversize/Jumbo grips can vary quite a bit, but in general will range around +1/8" to +3/8" larger in diameter. A standard method of measuring diameter will typically be 5cm below the butt end of the grip (usually where the upper hand wrist aligns with the grip). Similarly, Undersize and Junior grips will fall below 1" in diameter, sometimes nearing 0.8" or below. Because hands (and fingers) come in different shapes and sizes, it's important to try holding an installed grip before committing to changing the size of your golf grips for your entire set of clubs. The most popular golf grip size is Standard and Midsize, though in recent years many players have found Jumbo/Oversize grips help to reduce grip pressure. Use the menu on the left column.

Not to be confused with the outer diameter of a grip, there is a 2nd size measurement to keep in mind, which is the golf grip core size or inside diameter. The majority of golf grips have an inside diameter of 0.600" or 0.580". This is because most golf shafts have an outer diameter of this measurement as well. Commonly, club-builders will look to match the core size of the golf grip to the outer diameter of the golf shaft. In some cases, club-builders will want to install a 0.580" core size grip onto a 0.600" butt diameter shaft which will actually increase the outer diameter of the grip just slightly. In addition, there are grips that are smaller in diameter (usually for undersize or junior shafts ranging from 0.500" to 0.560"), or much larger (for bubble shafts, around 0.800" or higher).

Golf grips come in either round, ribbed, or alignment shapes. Round is the most popular shape for most grips, meaning you can orient the grip whichever way you prefer (some players like to have the logo of the grip facing up or down, or may choose a 360/no-logo grip). Ribbed grips have a small protruding ridge, designed to be oriented along the spine of the shaft. This rib, also called a "reminder", helps players feel where the bottom of the grip is, so they know how to properly place their hands. Recently, a more modern and prominent rib design has been introduced by some manufacturers, calling it an "Alignment" or "Calibrate" rib. These alignment grips feature an unmistakable ridge that runs along the full length of the grip.

4) Golf Grip Style / Material

Golf Grips come in many different styles but pretty much fall into one of these categories: Velvet, Composite, Wrap, Cord, and Hybrid (Cord + Rubber). The Velvet style grip was made popular by Golf Pride's flagship Tour Velvet line, which feature small repeating patterns of crosses using a rubber material. Velvet grips provides a light texture and traction for control without sacrificing feel. The Composite grip was made popular more recently with styles like the Winn Dri-tac and Golf Pride CP2, which feature a tacky and smooth surface that also provide visually enhancing patters and non-slip gripping. The Wrap style grip is actually a simulated 1-piece style but using a wrap design. The Winn Excel is a popular wrap style grip, as well as the Golf Pride Tour Wrap and Jumbomax Wrap grips. Cord grips have cord fabric interweaved through the surface of the grip. This provides traction and added firmness (feedback). The Hybrid style is a newer more modern style grip that utilizes both cord and rubber. The Golf Pride MCC Plus4 is one of the most notable Hybrid grips, which use a softer rubber for the lower hand and cord (for traction/control) in the upper hand.

5) Golf Grip Feel

Most golf grips will fall into one of three "feel" categories: Soft, Medium, and Firm. Grip feel is an important personal preference. Firm grips tend to provide more feedback to the hands at impact. Soft grips will absorb some of the impact and provide a more comfortable feel. Players that have arthritis or experience hand pain will play better with softer (and/or larger grips). If you prefer a soft grip, it's important to select a grip that has a stable core that will produce minimal torque so there is no twisting during the swing. The Golf Pride CP2 grips address this with a stabilizing inner core, as does the IOMIC LTC ("Low Torque Core") grips. If you prefer a firmer feel, many cord grips and velvet-style grips will provide this along with sharper feedback.

6) Golf Grip Weather Management

Golf grips have a limited life span. If you live in a wet weather or high moisture level climate, you'll want to make sure the golf grip you choose has high moisture management which will help it last longer and provide non-slip performance. Cord grip styles are great for wet weather playing, along with many composite material golf grips, such as the Winn Dri-Tac grips. IOMIC golf grips are also known to provide extended durability due to being 100% UV and water resistant, so they will not crack or fade from sun exposure. Lamkin also makes UV resistant grips, with their Genesis/Fingerprint material that provides longer lasting durability.

I have found the rotation in the golf swing to be vital. At one point, I was too steep in my backswing and relied on the timing of my hands, which often had me fighting a hook.

Now I am on a better plane, rotating through the shot, and allow the club to whip through the hitting zone by rotation and not by flipping of the hands. So my swing is now flatter, but not flat.

Pros and Cons of a Flat Swing?

Pros

- A golfer is already in a shallow position
- Does not take manipulation in the downswing
- Easier to stay on plane
- Able to rotate through the shot better without manipulation
- May help the golfer stay to the inside

Cons

- Can be difficult out of the rough
- Could cause the golfer to swing out of the top
- Golfer could get stuck in downswing

One of the keys to any golf swing is being shallow enough in the downswing to maximize contact, speed, and launch angle.

When a swing gets too steep, it could lead to disaster as the golfer often has to early extend, stall of flip at the ball as a result. Golf is a difficult game, but when you are too steep the golfer could really struggle with making solid, compression ball contact that sends the ball flying.

I have also seen many amateurs lift the club on their backswing, which makes them steep and then come out of the top causing the dreaded slice.

The flatter swing will allow the golf to continue to swing in a circle and hit the ball on the way out, promoting more of a draw swing versus an over the top slice swing.

Golfers with a steep backswing are still able to shallow it out, but it takes the hands falling down below the original backswing plane in order to shallow the ball.

When the hands and arms stay flatter on the backswing, the golfer is able to simply turn and rotate through the ball and keep the club on a shallow plane.

Some golfers, think Matt Wolff prefer that bit of a loop in the swing where the club is steep and then shallow it out. For the golfer who might only play once or twice a week this manipulation of the club and shallowing out method might be difficult to repeat when you aren't practicing every day!

Pro #3: Easier to stay on plane

Keeping the plane simple is recommended for the golfer who doens't have a ton of time to practice. Taking the arms back where the left arm is in line with the shoulder plan will keep the swing simple.

As someone with more of a steep swing, I find myself fighting to get the club shallow enough to make solid contact when I am struggling.

The golf swing that is very easy to repeat and keeps the club flat is the stack and tilt swing. This swing promotes the hands coming through the right bicep and keeping the club on a flatter plane.

If you get a deep enough turn with a flat plane, the golfer is able to rotate hard through the swing and utilize the bigger muscles to control the club face.

Golfers who are too steep, have to drop the club down and then rotate to be able to stay on the plane and keep the body from stalling and the hands flipping.

One of the biggest swing faults amongst many amateurs is not getting deep enough on the back swing (lack of shoulder turn) and then stalling or early extension in the downswing. This leads to the hands flipping and relying on the timing of the golf swing.

You might be amazed at the extra speed you are able to generate from properly rotating through the golf swing. As the hips and chest clear the club is able to really generate some speed at impact. If you are flipping early, you are losing your speed too early in the downswing.

If you ever wondered why you aren't consistent this may be the number one reason! Check out our post here on the 11 top reasons why a golf may be inconsistent!

Pro #5: May help the golfer stay to the inside
Of the 20 plus handicap golfers that i have seen, many struggle with the over the top move. They lift their arms up, lack turn and depth and then cut across the ball. Flattening out the swing will encourage you to hit the ball from the inside and start to create a push draw.

You have to be careful not to get too flat and then come ove the top.

Below are some cons to note.

Con 1: Can be difficult out of the rough
In really thick rough the flatter swings may struggle to be steep enough to make solid contact with the ball.

However, maybe you are consistent enough to keep it out of the steep rough by keeping the swing flatter and utilizing the rotation to stabilize the club face.

As mentioned above the flatter swing could result in the opposite action on the downswing and the golfer could have a slight over the top move from this flat position.

Many of the golfers that have steeper arms and hands int he swing, like that feel of dropping into the slot and then rotation through the shot. Be careful to have enough movement in the body while keep the hands back.

This will help reduce the over the top move.

As the golfer starts the downswing if the hands are too flat and then get flatter while the body starts to turn, you may find that you are "getting stuck."

This is a position where the body has cleared, the hands are stuck behind you and it often takes perfect timing that day to hit the ball straight.

Tiger Woods struggled with this position early in career and worked with Butch Harmon on freezer drills to help time up the downswing and the movements between his arm and his body.

CHAPTER TWO

Biggest Golf Swing Mistakes and How to Fix Them

With all the moving parts of a golf swing, there are a thousand things that can go wrong.

The driving range is a showcase of golf swing mistakes. But many golfers would improve dramatically just by eliminating big mistakes — foundational problems that instantly create a number of follow-on errors.

Here are some of the big mistakes you may be making with your golf swing.

Not Warming Up

Nothing will ruin your swing faster than trying to hit it 300 yards off the first tee without warming up. It's more common than you think.

This affliction is commonly observed on any local course on Saturday morning. Golfers either think they are too cool to warm up, or they don't know how.

Before the round, work through your bag by taking smooth swings with each club, starting with the wedges and progressing to fairway metals and driver. Limber, loose, warm muscles are the key to a relaxed, powerful swing.

Wrong Clubs

For some reason, many golfers have the impression that all clubs are the same. Perhaps they pick up a set on sale at a local department store, and then wonder why they are having problems with their swing.

As experienced golfers know, getting fitted correctly with the right clubs will go a long way toward eliminating many swing flaws without any additional effort by the golfer.

Swinging Too Hard

In the past few decades, the finesse aspect of golf has given ground to the power side of the game. Equipment manufacturers are partly to blame because much of their marketing talks about power and distance gains.

On the other hand, they are simply responding to what golfers say they want. Survey after survey shows that the number one thing golfers want is more distance and power. In an attempt to achieve these goals, golfers tend to swing way too hard and too fast.

While it is true that a faster swing will technically produce a longer shot, the ball must also be struck in the middle of the clubface. Average golfers do not have the skill to swing at tremendous speeds and hit the ball cleanly. By slowing down, you will give the swing time to happen in proper sequence. Your shots will be cleaner, you'll get healthy distance and much more consistency.

Gripping Too Tightly

Maybe it is a symptom of trying to swing too hard, but gripping too tightly on the club is a common error. It's as if golfers think someone is going to come up behind them and grab the golf club out of their hands and run off down the street with it. In some cases, you can see the veins popping out of the hands and wrists as they hold on with all their might.

The swing is an athletic motion and requires a loose, flowing action for optimal results. Gripping too tightly actually slows down the swing because the muscles are stiff and ineffective

If you are trying to throw a softball underhanded from behind home plate to the pitcher's mound, you wouldn't turn your body toward third-base. Yet that is what golfers do every day. Poor alignment is a major contributor to bad shots.

Often they line up their feet aiming directly at the target. In reality, the toes should be lined up parallel to the target line. Think of the target line and the stance line as the two rails on a railroad track. They are going in the same direction, but the left rail will always be aimed slightly to the left of the right rail, not at the exact same point.

The thing to keep in mind about alignment is that it must be continually maintained. Even professional golfers work hard at checking their alignment regularly. This is easily done by placing alignment rods or golf clubs on the ground during practice sessions. It helps to have a professional or friend check your alignment to make sure what you see is an accurate picture.

Golfers make things too hard for themselves. Sometimes they take the club back with a short backswing and then rush it forward at top speed. Other times, they take the club too far back and then with it forward, cutting off the follow-through.

Timing is a critical element in a productive golf swing. Timing is the art of allowing the sequence of positions to unfold naturally. A well-timed swing looks of fluid and unhurried. It moves slowly but steadily to the top of the backswing and then seems to pause while the lower body begins to turn toward the target, building up power ready to be released.

Good timing is created by lots of repetition. Golfers get into trouble when they do not practice their timing, and to fall back on bad habits once they get to the course. Daily drills that bolster a well-timed swing will pay off in spades on the next match.

Poor Grip

The grip is where the rubber meets the road. It is the only contact your body has with the club. When you have an incorrect grip, you set off an unfortunate sequence of events that can only result in disaster.

It should be firm, but not tight. Avoid holding the club too much in the palms. This reduces the ability of your wrists to operate freely. The club should be more in your fingers, which are the most sensitive areas of your hands.

While many golfers are able to place their rear hand — the right hand for right-handed golfers — on the club, they often have trouble with the leading hand. The most common error is a grip that is too weak, or turned too far to the left on top of the club. Another common error is a grip that is too strong, or turned too far to the right on top of the club. Often a grip that is too strong is the sign of a golfer trying to hit the ball too hard.

Relax and let your hands grip the club naturally so that the palms face each other, and are not turned too far to the left or right. The Vs between your finger and thumb should point at, or just outside, your right shoulder.

No acceleration

Have you ever been in a car with someone learning how to drive a manual stick shift? The driver does not press on the gas pedal enough while letting out the clutch, so the car jerks to a stop and stalls. A manual transmission requires that you accelerate smoothly for the clutch to engage with precision.

Your swing is similar.

Many amateurs tend to decelerate on the forward swing, rather than creating swing that smoothly builds up speed. The telltale sign of deceleration is when they look like they are scooping at the ball. This evidences a lack of trust in the swing.

Proper acceleration goes back to our previous discussion about timing. The club will build up tremendous power as it comes down and threw the ball, but only if you do not interrupt the free-flowing action.

Shooting at the Flag

Sure, if you are Bubba Watson, go ahead and take dead aim at that flag. The rest of should be content with hitting the center of the green and putting from there. Jack

Nicklaus credited his long, successful career to playing to the middle of the green and relying on his top-notch putting skills.

Putting will always have a higher success rate than chipping or sand play, so put it on the green, and get a solid par. Save the heroics for the company softball team.

Lack of a Full Shoulder Turn

The real power in a golf swing comes from leverage. Golfers lose this leverage when they fail to make a full shoulder turn.

Commonly, they make a fake shoulder turn where they bend the left arm in an attempt to extend the backswing. This cuts off any chance to use the power and torque stored in the wind-up of the shoulders.

Swinging Over the Top

You may have heard the term "over the top" many times but not fully understood its meaning.

Remember that the swing is moving both up and down as well as back and forth. At the top of the swing, amateur golfers begin to turn their shoulders on the forward swing before they give their arms a chance to fall down on an inside path. The club swings wide over the proper swing path like an airliner banking before final approach, and then cuts across the target line.

Hitting the target: The golfer's guide

Golf is an individual sport played by hitting a ball with a club from a tee into a hole. The object is to get the ball into the hole with the least number of swings or strokes of the club. Golf is a hugely popular sport that is enjoyed by people of all ages. Golf is often played competitively, but can also be played for relaxation and just to enjoy the outdoors.

Basic Shots You Should Know

There are parts of golf that will elude you your entire life, but certain fundamentals are essential. You have to be able to hit a driver off the tee with a fair amount of confidence. You have to be able to hit an iron off the ground, and get out of a greenside bunker. You have to know a few basic short shots around the green, and be able to keep your cool when things get ugly.

When you have a short shot to the green, you're going to hit either a chip or a pitch. What's the difference between the two? A chip shot stays low and runs along the ground, and a pitch flies higher and doesn't roll as much. Use a chip when you don't have to carry the ball over an obstacle, like deep rough or a bunker, and you have a lot of green between you and the hole. Use a pitch when you have to carry over something or need to stop the ball faster. The extra height on a pitch shot causes the ball to land softer and stop faster.

Get out of a bunker every time

The greenside bunker shot is the one shot in golf where you don't actually hit the ball: You swing the clubhead into the sand behind the ball, and the sand pushes it out. For that reason, you have to swing quite a bit harder than you might expect; the sand really slows down the clubhead. Here's the basic technique: Using your sand wedge, stand so the ball is even with your front instep, twist your feet in for stability, and focus on a spot about two inches behind the ball. Swing the club back about halfway then down and through that spot behind the ball.

Keep turning your body so your chest faces the target at the finish.

Use your athleticism

Beginning golfers often get so tied up in the instructions for making the swing that they lose their athletic instincts. Golf might be more mental than other sports, but the swing is still a dynamic, athletic movement. Here are a few sports images that will help you: At address, stand like a defender in basketball, with your legs lively and your weight balanced left to right and front to back. On the backswing, think of a quarterback rearing back to make a pass: Arm stretched back and body coiled from top to bottom. And on the downswing, be like a hockey player hitting a slap shot, with your wrists staying firm and your hands leading the clubhead into the ball.

Don't fear the big dog

You might think the driver is more than you can handle right now: It's the longest club in your bag, and the head is gigantic. The truth is, built into that big clubhead is more forgiveness for mis-hits than you get with any other club. Have a few driver keys to rely on.First, tee the ball nice and high. Second, take the club back smoothly and make a full body turn, getting your back to face the target. Third, swing through the ball; just let it get in the way of the clubhead through impact. Last, hold your finish. If you can finish in balance, you've swung at a speed you can control.

Lost your way? Go back to chipping

Learning golf can at times be overwhelming. When you feel frustrated, go back to hitting short chip shots. The chipping swing is the basis of the entire swing; it's the full swing in miniature. And with the chipping motion being so short and slow, you can more easily understand what's happening. To play a chip, position the ball back in your stance, put more weight on your left foot, and swing equal lengths back and through without hinging your wrists on either side. Once you get a feel for the chip, swing a little longer by hinging the club upward with your wrists and letting your weight shift back and through. In no time you'll build a feel for the full swing.

No doubt, the right equipment always helps, but it's not as if you'll need to empty your savings account to get started. Instead, focus on finding the sort of equipment that will allow you to develop your imperfect skills with minimal expense. There'll be plenty of time to go after the latest, hot products on the market (and when you do, make sure you start your search with one of our top 100 clubfitters, but at the beginning, make learning -- and not buying -- your priority.

You only need a few clubs

You're allowed to carry as many as 14 clubs in your bag, but you won't need nearly that many when you're first learning. Instead, start with a driver, a putter, a sand wedge (it's the club that has an "S" on the sole or a loft of 54 to 56 degrees) and supplement those with a 6-iron, an 8-iron, a pitching wedge, and a fairway wood or hybrid with 18-21 degrees of loft. These are the clubs that are the most forgiving and easiest to get airborne. You can find used and new titanium drivers for as little as $75 and putters for much less than online, but most larger golf and general sporting goods stoes also offer racks of discounted and/or used clubs.

Don't guess -- try before you buy

If you're an absolute beginner looking to buy clubs, go to a larger golf shop or driving range and ask to try a 6-iron with a regular-flex and a stiff-flex shaft. (Generally, the faster and more aggressive the swing, the more you will prefer a shaft that is labeled "S" for stiff.) One of the two should feel easier to control. That's the shaft flex you should start with for all your clubs. Once you get serious about the game and are able to make consistent contact, a clubfitting will enable you to get the most out of your equipment.

The more loft, the better

Unless you're a strong and well-coordinated athlete experienced with stick and ball sports (baseball, softball, hockey, tennis, for example), opt for woods that have more loft. Why? The extra loft generally means it will be easier to get the ball in the air and also can reduce sidespin so shots fly straighter. So go for drivers with at least 10 degrees of loft and fairway woods that start at 17 degrees, not 15 degrees.

Take advantage of clubs made for beginners

Some types of clubs are easier to hit than others. For one thing, you're better off with hybrids instead of 3-, 4-, and 5-irons. And irons with wider soles (the bottom part of an iron) will alleviate the tendency for the club to stick in the ground when you hit too far behind the ball. Also, with more weight concentrated in the sole, the iron's center of gravity will be lower and this will help shots launch on a higher trajectory. Generally, a more forgiving iron will feature a sole that measures about the width of two fingers (from front edge to back). If an iron's sole measures less than one finger width, you only should be playing it if you're paid to do so. To find the right iron for you, browse through the super game improvement irons on our Hot List.

Choose The Right Ball

Buy balls on a sliding scale based on how many you lose in a round. If you've never played before or lose two sleeves or more a round, buy balls that cost around $20 a dozen (if you can't decide between one brand over another, try putting a few to see how they feel coming off the putter face). When you cut the number of lost balls back to maybe three to five balls a round, buy balls that cost less than $30 a dozen. Only if you're losing less than a sleeve a round should you consider the $40 a dozen balls. For a complete rundown of golf balls, see our ball Hot List.

Learning To Play

The hardest part about golf can be getting started. Ask yourself a few questions. First, why do you want to play? Is it for work or social reasons? Maybe then you need only some basic instruction and patient friends. Perhaps you're looking to jump in headfirst in hopes of getting better fast. If so, there's plenty of top-level instruction out there. Next, how much are you willing to put into it? That goes for time and the money. Point is, there's a huge difference between wanting to ride around and have some laughs and being a serious player.

Everyone wants to see how far they can hit a golf ball, but when you go to the driving range, resist the temptation to immediately start ripping drivers. Yes, you might crank a couple, but swinging for maximum distance will throw you out of sync -- and fast. Start out by hitting one of your wedges or short irons, warming up your golf muscles with half-swings. Then increase the length and speed of your swings, and move on to your middle irons. Work your way up to the driver, and after you hit some balls with it, go back to a short iron or wedge. This will help you keep your tempo and tension level in check. Read David Leadbetter's advice on warming up before you play.

Learn the short shots

Roughly half of your strokes come within 50 yards of the green. That means you probably should spend half of your practice time with your wedges and putter. This might sound boring, but the good news is, you can practice your short game in your own back yard -- even in your TV room. Put out some buckets in your yard at various distances and try to pitch balls into them. Give yourself good lies and bad lies, just like you get on the course. As for putting, your carpet might not play as fast as the greens, but you can still practice aiming and rolling balls through doorways and into furniture legs. Here are some more bright ideas on practice.

When in doubt, go back to basics

Golf can really get you thinking too much. There's a lot of information out there, and the most mind-numbing part can be the instruction. When you're a new golfer, you can't help but read it and watch it, but too much can be, well, too much. When you find yourself getting burned out from too much swing thinking, go back to basics. Try to get yourself into a good setup -- check your ball position and posture -- then make a relaxed swing all the way to a full finish. Over-thinking creates tension, so be aware of your stress level: Waggle the club a little at address and try to make a smooth move off the ball. Nothing ruins your chances faster than snatching the club back.

When You're Ready For The Golf Course

So now that you've got some clubs and you've learned the basics of the golf swing, you're thinking about testing yourself on an actual golf course. Great, but it's not as if you should step right onto the same course the pros play. If you want to make sure your early experiences on the golf course are positive ones, it's best to know your limitations, then build yourself up. Here's what to keep in mind.

Start small

Golf is hard enough without needing eight shots just to get to the green. Start on a par 3 or "executive" course before you try an 18-hole championship course. On a par-3 course, all the holes are par 3s -- that is, usually less than 200 yards. Executive courses typically have multiple par-3 holes and their par 4s and 5s are shorter than what you'd find on a championship course. Give yourself some time to get acclimated here before taking on a bigger challenge.

Play three holes

In a way, golf its own kind of an endurance sport, and you need to build yourself up to playing 18 holes. Consider starting by playing three holes of a nine-hole course late in the afternoon when the course is less crowded and rates are cheaper. The course might not charge a three-hole rate, so just play until you start getting frustrated, then come back another day.

Choose the right course

Don't start on Bethpage Black, or any course that's going to have you discouraged before you reach the first green. A good beginner course is flat, short and doesn't have many hazards or forced carries -- that is, waste areas or hazards you have to hit over to get to the fairway. There'll be plenty of time to test yourself on tougher layouts, but for now, give yourself a chance to gather some positive momentum.

Move on up

Forget about ego, and feel free to play from the forward set of tees. Playing the course at 5,500 yards or less will save you time, frustration and golf balls. And you'll be in good company: there's a nationwide push for recreational golfers of all levels to be playing courses from shorter distances.

Most golf courses ask that you finish 18 holes in four-and-a-half hours, but you can do better than that. One way to maintain a decent pace is to limit yourself to a certain number of strokes per hole. (We suggest a maximum of seven strokes per hole.) As a beginning golfer, there's nothing wrong with picking up your ball if you're holding your playing partners up.

Those Pesky Rules

Yes, it's true, the Rules of Golf is 182 pages long and understanding many of the game's 34 rules is important. But don't worry. Most golfers, including those guys who turned their noses up at playing with a newcomer like you, have very little knowledge of how to play the game correctly. You'd be surprised by how many golfers just make rules up as they go, so don't fret if you're not sure about what's OK and what's a violation. Just remember these key points and you'll do fine for now.

Don't move your ball

Unless you're on a putting green, don't move your ball under any circumstance. Play it as it lies unless it's interfered with by an obstruction (think man-made object

-- yardage marker, beer can, etc.). And if you're not sure what an obstruction is, ask the head pro or an experienced golfer. On the putting green, you have to mark the ball's position before lifting it, usually with a coin or a small ball marker.

Stick with your own ball

If you see a ball that's not your own, you may think, "Hey, free ball!" But what you should do is leave it. Believe it or not, you're not the only golfer on the course who is hitting his ball to unintended locations, so it could be another player's ball from another hole. And speaking of which.

It's (mostly) OK to play from another hole

If your shot lands in another fairway, you can play the ball as it lies as long as that fairway is not designated as out of bounds (white stakes or lines). If you don't see white stakes or lines, you can play back to the hole you're playing. Just don't interfere with players on that particular hole. Let them play through unless they give you permission to go first. If your ball is outside the out-of-bounds markers, take a one-stroke penalty and play another shot from the spot you just hit from.

Only take five minutes to look for a ball

If you hit a shot and you can't find the ball after five minutes of searching, take a one-stroke penalty and play another shot from as close as possible to the last spot you played from. This might require you to drop a ball. If so, extend your hand at shoulder height over that area, simply drop it, then play from there.

Play within the golf course

If you ever hit a shot out-of-bounds (white stakes or lines), you have to replay a shot from as close as possible to where you just hit and add a stroke penalty to your score. So, for instance, if you teed off and hit a shot out of bounds, take a stroke penalty and play your third shot again from the tee.

There's a reason why you can't accelerate through the ball like a touring pro and it's not because you weren't handed a golf club in your crib. A key component to making an efficient, powerful and correct golf swing is having a body that's able to do it. Strong hip muscles, flexible hamstrings and a stable back are just a few reasons why tour pros are tour pros and most of the rest of us are, well, not. If you want to play well, and play this game for the rest of your life, you have to exercise and pay specific attention to the muscles that will allow you to do it. Start with these areas and you'll be in great "golf shape" in no time.

Walk, don't ride

Whenever you can, no matter how tiring it might seem, walk instead of riding in a golf cart. And carry your clubs when you can. A seven-mile walk with clubs on your back might seem daunting now, but it will get easier the more you do it. And if you're worried your golf bag is too heavy, our golf bag Hot List features several great lightweight bags with pop-up stands.

Save long-hold stretches for after the round or at night. Before the round, do dynamic stretches that prep your muscles for the golf swing. For instance, swinging a leg back and forth like you're kicking a ball. Make this kicking motion 10 times for each leg trying to kick higher each time. To see a couple of more dynamic stretches you can do before your round, see these examples provided by Golf Digest fitness expert Randy Myers and Dustin Johnson.

Almost all food served at golf courses is trouble. Burgers, dogs, granola bars, chips -- they may seem appealing at the moment, but they're not going to help your performance. The best foods to eat for a round of golf are lean protein (such as chicken or turkey) and complex carbohydrates (such as all-bran cereal or a banana). You should eat before the round and again at the turn, or on the back nine, to maintain energy and concentration. And drink lots and lots of water. If you're urine is not clear in color, you are likely dehydrated.

The most important muscles in the golf swing are located from the top of your knees to under your chest. Focus on them when you weight train and you'll have a powerful swing and stay injury free. Squats, lunges, and planks.

If you're sore after a round, ice is OK to reduce swelling, but only apply to the sore area for 15 minutes per hour, max. In the morning, apply heat (a warm shower will help) or heat wraps and consider taking pain relievers such as ibuprofen, acetaminophen, aspirin or naproxen sodium before playing. But do so only with a doctor's blessing since the masking of pain can lead to further injury.

Learning how to play may be the most important part of becoming a golfer, but not to be overlooked is knowing what to wear. Your attire matters for a variety of reasons:

because most golf courses enforce some kind of dress code (some stricter than others); because you'll be spending at least four hours outdoors; and because, frankly, who doesn't want to look sharp? With that in mind, we provide five pointers to make sure you're outfitted right for the course.

Pick the right collared shirt

Most courses, even public ones, require that men wear a collared polo (women are more often allowed to play without a collared top). There are two main types of collared shirts: those made of cotton, and others made of more technical fabrics. If you feel more comfortable in a traditionally-cut polo, stick with cotton. But if it'll be hot on the golf course, collared shirts made of technical fabrics, such as those made by Adidas, Nike and Callaway, will help keep you dry by wicking moisture away from your skin.

Stick to khakis

Hands down, these are the most comfortable pants to play in, especially since khaki fabric is more breathable than ever before. And you won't find a golf course that doesn't allow you to wear khaki pants. Most courses, save for a few traditional private clubs, now allow shorts as well, although some are iffy on cargo shorts. As for jeans, best to leave those at home. Even if a course allows them, they're uncomfortable for golf.

Prepare yourself for the elements

If all goes well, you won't be spending your entire round punching your ball out from under trees, so shielding yourself from the sun will be important. A basic baseball cap never fails, and when it's time to buy sunglasses for golf, make sure the lens blocks UVA and UVB rays, and that they wrap around your eyes to offer complete coverage. Of course, golf is played in all kinds of weather. You'll need a good rain jacket for wet conditions, and you should always carry a dry towel to keep your grips dry.

For starters, go with sneakers, not golf shoes

Hold off on purchasing golf shoes until you become really serious about the game. Stick with sneakers, which you'll be able to use on and off the course. Since you'll want to stay as level to the ground as possible, make sure you don't wear running sneakers, which have too much cushion under the heal of your foot.

A must-have accessory for all golfers. You'll need to apply sunblock 30 minutes before your round and again at the turn, since the SPF in sunblock wears off after a couple of hours. (See our skin cancer guide here). Look for a sunblock with an SPF of at least 30. Also, try spray sunblocks when you reapply during your round, since you can apply it without making your hands slippery, and don't forget to apply a lip balm with SPF.

CONCLUSION

How frustrating is it to try everything imaginable to lower your golf score, yet continue to fail miserably? Isn't it agonizing when your golf game seems to be improving tremendously in one round, but then it falls apart in the next round? Are you spending countless hours trying to figure out how to improve your swing, yet you don't seem to be seeing any results? The good news is…you've come to the right place. This book can change all of that for you in just a few minutes, as it has have done for 106,000 other golfers just like you, in more than 27 countries.

www.ingramcontent.com/pod-product-compliance
Lightning Source LLC
Chambersburg PA
CBHW061329120726
48001CB00002B/756